DEDICATION

This book is dedicated to my loving parents who did not give me a hard time when I decided to leave my "good job," to recreate the life I wanted for myself.

My close tribe of friends who have continued to encourage me through this journey, and to every person of color who thinks that their influence in the world is not enough.

Let's create the spaces that we so deserve in this world.

So You Want To Become A Travel Influencer?

Listen.

The goal of creating this book is to share with you how to become a profitable Travel Influencer of Color. At the time of writing this, I have been "in the game" of creating a business from my influencer over four years. And up until this point, there is no resource on the market that is sharing with you the business of Influence as a person of color. And yes, how you pursue a create a company as a POC is, in fact, different from a non-POC.

It ain't easy.

But it's rewarding. And before I give you the Blueprint, I have first to tell you how I got started, the ups and downs, and what I wish I knew before making this shift.
Let's get into it.

MY STORY

Imagine.

A twenty-something with the 'ideal life.'
By twenty-six, I had graduated with honors with an MBA in Marketing, moved to the tri-state area, and landed a lucrative and promising career at a Fortune Top 50 corporation. I had the perfect apartment, in the ideal location, with the excellent job, making more money than I'd ever seen before - I was 'ballin"!

Well, so I thought.

After a few years of working in Corporate America, I realized that the Rat Race was going to kill me slowly. I will never forget this day. It was my turning point. One morning after a presentation, my heart starting beating too fast, my hands trembling, it was becoming unbearably hot, and I just knew that the walls were going to close in on me right there in the conference room. So, I went to the bathroom to breathe and have a moment to myself. I leaned my back against the coolness of the wall; slide down, and started sobbing. Uncontrollably. I wanted to scream. I wanted to cry. And I completely wanted out of my "perfect life." I had no idea what was wrong with me. After all, the presentation was stellar, and I was "living my best life."

This wasn't normal. After a scheduled doctor's appointment, I would then discover that I was suffering from Anxiety Disorder and Depression.

Hair loss, the random trembles, constant fatigue, loss of interest in things I once loved, and drastic changes of my healthy habits, was in fact, not a symptom of "working too hard."

Again, how could someone who "has it all," be so depressed? "Perhaps I am ungrateful?" was what I often asked myself. So to maintain my facade of "having it all," I silently went to see a therapist every Wednesday on my lunch break - for a year. I felt like a fraud, yet going to therapy taught to dive deeper into my true desires. So much so, that I decided to leave my "good job."

I sold and gave away most of my belongings in my charming apartment in the trendy neighborhood, packed up my car, and headed back home to Florida.

A month later, I booked the cheapest flight of my life and flew to Bangkok for $15.30 (travel hacking!)! Where I started my backpacking journey for three months through South East Asia.

It was the most fantastic experience and a pivotal turning point in my life.

And of course, I know what you're thinking. Yes, my family and friends thought I had completely lost it. I left a six-figure career, amazing social life, great lifestyle, and so much more – for what? To seek happiness and fulfilled?

The one thing that has always made me feel alive, vibrant, and curious - was travel. It all started in high school, when the magnet program I was in, sent us to China for a month. A few months later, my Honors class sent us to Italy. From then on, I was hooked.

While backpacking, I created my travel blog: RachelTravels.com, to document my journey from depression to who I was becoming as a woman. I also decided to record some of the conversations I had with those I met along the way, highlight the destinations, and share how I was able to afford to travel around the world solo.

I began to share these stories, blog posts, and images across social media and among online friends. My angle was to be as open and transparent as possible about my travel journey and my road from depression and anxiety, into creating a new life for myself. Through my candidness, a tribe of people began to follow me, resonate with the journey, and look forward to what I share.

Listening to their challenges and concerns, I leveraged my degrees in Marketing and my corporate expertise in Digital Marketing, to create online products, services, and consultations. Making sure to be a continual learner, I learned how to optimize my experience in travel, marketing, and the business of influence, and earn an income on actively and passively; an income, which allows me to travel the world and live abroad.

Fast-forward over four years later; I now have a successful brand created from my travels and the authority created from sharing valuable content from the journeys. Through branding, positioning, consistency, networking, and a few other elements, I became a Travel Influencer.

This influence has allowed me to work with major brands like Norwegian Airlines and do projects with amazing destinations like Finland, Guadeloupe, Thailand, and more. I've been featured in major publications like HuffPost, USA Today, Rolling Out, and so many more credible sources. Lastly, and most importantly, make a living from it.

So listen.
I am not merely saying this to brag, but to share how I did it and you can too.

This book was created for any person of color who desires to recreate their lives and make a living from building authority around your passion for traveling the world. This booked is designed to show you how to create, leverage, and profit from your love of travel. This was written to show you how to be a profitable Travel Influencer.

And while "Influencer" is a super sexy term and it looks fantastic on social media, there is a lot of work that goes into becoming a profitable Travel Influencer. Note, the keyword here: profitable.

Anyone can create social media accounts, post tons of photos of their travels, accumulate thousands of followers, and call himself or herself a "Travel Influencer." But the number of these people who are making an income from their influence is likely quite small.

If you're willing to do the work, desire to be a continual learner, and can be consistent, then you can do this.

The Downside Of 'Influence'

It was quite a debate on whether or not this section should be included in the book. While this is a resource, it is essential that to understand the "dark side" of Influence. That isn't to say that there is some spookiness in the industry, but there are some aspects of creating this type of business that you should understand:

(1) **People Are Petty**: Let's put ten on twenty. Some of your favorite "Influencers" are mean, rude, and petty. They value their number of followers over creating synergy among their colleagues. There are too many examples to share, however, as you begin this journey, find other Travel Influencers that are also starting on this journey and commit to helping each other. As people of color, there is strength in numbers. We are tasked with changing the narrative of how the world perceives travel in diverse markets. Do not let the number of followers on social media validate who you are as a brand and as a person.

(2) **You Will Have To Work 10x Harder**: If you're a person of color reading this, the statement is self-explanatory. There is still a lot of proving and change. The industry is slowing getting there, but that is why we need more people like you, to help shift the story behind how people of color travel the world.

(3) **Life As An Influencer Doesn't Pay That Well**: While you may hear some people 'claim' they are making six-figures as an

Influencer, most of them are not. Through this book, you will learn multiple ways to create income that will help you move toward the six-figure mark, without relying on solely working with brands to make a profit.

(4) **Being An "Influencer" Is Trendy**: Be honest with yourself. If your desire to become a Travel Influencer is based on recognition, validations, and looking "cool" on social media, then reconsider! The word "influencer" may be something completely different in a few years. And while it can be amazing, it takes entirely too much work and consistency to create a growing brand, to call yourself an "Influencer."

Now that we got that all out of the way, are you ready?

Let's get started.

CHAPTER ONE

What Is A Travel Influencer

What It Is & What It Is Not:

'Travel Influencer' is this super sexy term that's floating around the 'net.

According to the Cambridge Dictionary, "Influencer" is defined as, "someone who affects or changes the way that other people behave, for example, through the use of social media."

It is utilizing your expertise in a particular area, to create an online presence to 'persuade' people to do things like:
- See specific destinations
- Learn new skills
- Experience new activities
- Download apps
- Try new software
- Make purchasing decisions
- And so on

In simple terms, people look to your guidance, advice, and direction to make a move.

Often, it seems as though being a Travel Influencer is super exciting. The free trips, partnering with brands, making money online, and living life by your own rules, is very enticing. And it is all very exhilarating and fun, but the amount of work that goes into it is that part that many do not discuss.

And it is. Or shall I say, it can be.

You're likely reading this because you desire to be a Travel Influencer. However, before laying out the moving parts and pieces, let us first set a few expectations.
Understand this:

(1) **It is Hard Work**: Creating an authentic, transparent, and profitable travel brand will take a lot of work to build. Don't you think just because you have a great social media profile that it automatically qualifies as a business or qualifies you as a travel Influencer? Nope! It just means you have beautiful and fun photos on social media! That's it. This does not mean that companies want to work with you, that people trust your opinion, and it certainly doesn't say that people are willing to buy from you.

(2) **It Takes An Investment**: If you are not willing to invest time, resources, or money to build a profitable brand as an online Travel Influencer, then hang it up. It doesn't take a substantial investment of money to get started (it only took me about $350), but you must be willing to be committed to the process. The placement of time and consistency it takes will cost you the most.

(3) **You're Not Going to Blow Up Immediately**: Beyoncé, Oprah, nor Michael Jordan as brands, weren't made overnight. Neither will you. So relax, stay consistent, and continue to learn and grow.

Now that we have set a few expectations let us discuss the four elements you should focus on as you build your travel brand.

The 4 Things To Focus On As A Travel Influencer

Often, when people start their journey to becoming a Travel Influencer, they tend to worry about and focus on the wrong things at the very beginning of building their brands.

You Should Avoid The Following:
- Stressing out over the brand logo
- Which platform your website will be hosted
- How your site should look
- What colors your brand will have
- How your social media profile should look

If you're thinking about any of these for over a week and a half, you could potentially be wasting a ton of time, energy, and effort.

As you are getting started building your brand, here are the four areas you should focus on from the very beginning:

#1: Create Consistent & Valuable Content:

Yes. You have likely heard this before, and you will read it repeatedly in this book; however, it is essential that you be focused on creating quality content consistently.

TRUTH BOMB: This may hurt to hear. But this is as real as it gets. Most people are not consistent. Think about all of the times we have started a diet, workout routine, or other habit and fall off in a few weeks or days. The key to consistency is passion, drive, motivation, and discipline. Remember, this is a marathon, not a sprint.

It is easy to start a habit where you may show up online for a month straight with great content, then drop off altogether. Then, come back a month or two later and do it again.

This is like being in an emotionally unavailable relationship with your audience. And we all know those suck.

You could potentially put yourself in a position where your audience does not trust you because you seem "flaky. They have no idea why, what, or when to expect anything from you.

Keep this in mind. It is important when we begin to discuss generating sales and making passive income.

When it comes to working and partnering with brands; if you are not consistent with your brand and content, they (the partnering Brand) will quickly assume you will not be consistent and produce quality for them. And you always want brands to consider you as a dependable Influencer. Always.

#2: Ask Your Audience What They Want
When creating content, you want to focus on what your audience's challenges, issues, and desires.

Never, ever assume you know what your audience wants.

It is a hard lesson to learn, so take heed.

There's nothing worse than creating fantastic content, you post it, and then - crickets. No one reads it, resonates with it, or makes a purchase.

This happened to me early on when I first started my travel blog. Coming from a tech background, I wrote an article about the "best apps for travel" for that year. It was a complete dud. Not because it wasn't valuable information, but it just was not a challenge and/or concern that my audience had about travel. When I wrote a post about how I was able to travel around South East Asia for months on a small budget that got a lot more traction on the site.

No matter how small your audience, ask them what sort of challenges they're having; ask if they'd be interested if you created a particular type of content – then, build from there.

Some strategies to understand what your audience wants from you are:
- Survey them by posing questions on your Social Media feed
- Create Polls
- Ask Them Engaging Questions
- Ask Them to Respond to Posts + Videos
- Go Live or Do 'Stories' and ask them to reply if they're interested in learning more
- Email your list of subscribers and ask them to reply with insights or challenges they are experiencing

With social media, it's as simple as positioning an image, video, or poll and see what type of responses you get within 24 hours.

The way I created the course, Book It For A Buck: Travel Hacking 101, was by just asking my audience on social media, "Hey! If I created a resource sharing how I can travel cheaply all over the world, would you be interested?" There was an overwhelming response, so I created the course from there.

#3: Focus on Organically Building Your Following:

It is enticing, the idea of going from zero to thousands of social media followers quickly.
Growing your travel brand (or any brand) is a marathon, not a sprint.

Yes, you can purchase followers and likes, but at the end of the day, it's just not real. When it comes to brand partnerships, they typically use tools and software to run analytics on your social media accounts. If they find that your followers are bots, then be assured that the brands no longer trust you or desires to collaborate with you.

Because social media, policies, and algorithms change rapidly, make sure you stay on top of new information and insights on how to grow your brand utilizing social media the right way.

Pick one or two social media platforms and focus on studying that platform and build your credibility and following on them.

#4 Engage With Your Audience:

Being engaging with your audience is the quickest and easiest way to begin growing your "know, like, and trust factor (KLTF)."
We will define and go deeper into the KLTF further in the book; however, there are several ways to grow your KLTF:

• **Responding To Every Comment And Question**: Yes, it is time-consuming but find the joy in creating authentic engagement. This is how you build real, solid, relationships and levels of trust from a digital perspective. Not only does this help develop a personal connection with your audience, but also helps you to remain 'relevant' in the algorithm of the social media platform you will be using.

• **Ask Your Audience Engaging Questions That Make Them Eager to Respond To You**: One of the questions that got the highest amount of engagement on my social media was, "What is the weirdest thing you've eaten abroad?" It is a simple question. Many people were eager to share some of the weird and crazy things they've eaten while traveling. It was a great way to boost engagement, connect with Followers, and gain a level of "like" from them. Not to mention the new followers from the spike in engagement on the social media platform.

• **Make Sure You Respond Within The First Hour**: This can be difficult, but don't allow over twenty-four hours to go by before responding. It is a best practice to respond to comments within the hour. The social media algorithms are tricky and forever changing, but it is likely that if you have waited over twenty- four hours to respond, you have missed the momentum and wave to have your content seen by new viewers.

<u>HACK</u>: A strategy that has worked well for my Brand, is to schedule out my posts that require engagement at the same time daily. This way, I am in place and know that I need to dedicate time to responding and interacting with my social media following.

The Importance of Being A Travel Influencer of Color:

There are a vast need and gap for brands to tap into diverse markets. In fact, according to an article written on INC.com [1], if brands DO NOT start creating specific and targeted campaigns for diverse markets, they are going to see a massive drop in profits and popularity. This is a fantastic opportunity for you to come in and help these brands shift and change the way their market their products and services to various demographics.

Let's explore some of the statistics that will better be able to paint the picture of what the spending power of diverse markets looks like:

• Fifty- four percent of Asian- American women have traveled outside the continental U.S. in the last three years, which is 67% higher than non-Hispanic white women[II].

• In 2016, Black Americans spent over $56B in travel[III].

• Marketers have a massive opportunity for growth in the Hispanic market, as Latina women are increasing as breadwinners in the household and impacting buying decisions[IV].

With the increase in spending, especially in travel, there is a need for an increase in representation, awareness, and more message positioning. Here is where you, as a Travel Influencer, can genuinely help these brands tap into the diversity and unique markets, not limited to sub-groups, cultures, races, etc.

What is important to remember, is defining and knowing your audience444.

In the next chapter, will dive deeper into finding your target audience.

To begin, you want to start thinking about:
• Who you are serving
• Why you are helping them
• What impact it will have on your audience in the long-term

How to Get Over Yourself and Overwhelm:

There is so much information out there about building a brand online, growing a following on social media, and making money online. Many do not address the frustration and overwhelm that comes with information overload.

It can take days, weeks, months, and even years to consume enough of what you need to move the needle in your brand-building journey. And with all that is happening in our daily lives, it is difficult to make time to consume a ton of information. Naturally, this can cause overwhelm and frustration.

Let's discuss how to manage overwhelm and frustration as you are building a profitable travel Influencer brand.

First things first, there will be a need for a mindset shift.

It seems as though people desire this overnight success of your brand taking off immediately.

Stop it. You would be putting unrealistic expectations and pressure on yourself and the growth of your brand.

The next step is to create a plan and strategy for your brand.

Develop growth goals. Create a plan of action on how you plan to achieve those goals.

Just as in life, there are seasons in your business. There will be a season of building, a season of massive growth, a season of stagnation, and seasons of flourishing.

Shift your mindset into understanding it is only a season, and just like in life, seasons change.

Your journey toward building a profitable brand as a Travel Influencer will ebb and flow.

There are going to be high moments, and there are going to be some low moments, there will be some moments where you feel like you're just floating or you feel stagnant. Don't panic. It's normal.

Set realistic goals and intentions for your brand. If that means you can only dedicate one hour to your brand a day, then make it the most productive one-hour possible.

Pace yourself.

Stay focused on what will move the needle in your business.

It's okay if you get frustrated. It's okay if you feel overwhelmed. Take a break and breathe through it.

Shifting your mindset is often left out or not reinforced when it comes to brand building.

As you begin to build your brand, you must evaluate, unlearn, and relearn your thoughts and programming around worthiness, motivation, money, disciple, and resilience.

Now that we have mindset covered let's focused on the most critical aspect of building your profitable brand as a Travel Influencer; and that is understanding, identifying, and nailing your target audience.

With 1000% transparency, note that is has taken me years to shift my mindset around what to charge, worthiness to be chosen for specific projects, and so on. Currently, it is still a work in progress. Stay encouraged and take time to tap into your limiting beliefs. Once you are aware and acknowledge those, you can find the right resources to help you push through them and continue to flourish in creating your business of influence.

CHAPTER TWO

Understanding Your Audience & Niche

Why You Can't Be Everything to Everybody:

The quicker you hear, understand, and embrace this - the easier it will be for you to transcend and evolve as a Travel Influencer.

You cannot be everything to everybody.

And thank goodness for it! Think about how much pressure it would be on you to try to please millions of people.

When it comes down to you honing in on your niche, it is best to get specific and targeted.

Not so niched down and targeted that you pigeon-hole yourself, but enough to where you are serving a diverse but specific group of people who need, want and desire your content and services.

Here is a quick example:
Niche + Targeted: "I serve Millennial women of color who are aspiring or beginner scuba divers."

This niche market works because it is targeted to a specific demographic (millennial, women of color) and it tells what their interests are (new or aspiring scuba divers).
Too Broad: "I serve millennial women."

Do you know the broad interests of the millions of millennial women exist worldwide? That is a lot of ground to cover, especially when just starting a brand.

Pigeon-Hole: "I serve Millennial women of color, who are married with children and live in Rhome, Texas and are aspiring or beginner scuba divers."

We were all good until we got so specific that it does not leave room to expand or serve a wide(r) range. For starters, Rhome, Texas is landlocked and has a population of about 1500+ people. The likelihood that your demographic is even in Rhome, Texas is very slim.

How To Find Your Niche (The Actionable Methods):

Starting, you may not know precisely who your target audience may be. The easiest way when starting is to choose those that you want to serve and impact. Then, do this test below:
Here is a quick "test" to see if your niche makes sense for your brand:

Are your answers YES to the below statements? You should be able to hit the first two points. It is best if you answer YES to all three.

<u>Do You Have:</u>
- A topic you'll enjoy working in and be consistent with creating content?
- A problem you are or can become more knowledgeable in?
- Is this an issue that has profit potential? (This means there are similar products in the marketplace that consumers are already purchasing.)

The way you define and test to make sure this is the correct audience is to following your data and analytics, which we will dive deeper into later in the book.

How To "Niche Down" And Be Highly Targeted:

According to the Cambridge Dictionary, a niche is defined as, "an area or position that is exactly suitable for a small group of the same type."

Then you have a sub-niche, which is a smaller piece of that niche.

For example, our niche is going to be "travel," but your sub-niche may be, "solo travel for women."

To take it a step further, which is where I want you to concentrate, is to do what is called "niche down" one more level, which is to create a sub-niche of your sub-niche! Don't get confused; follow this example below:

Our sub-sub-niche (where we came down one more level) is: "women of color."

<u>Let's Recap:</u>
- **Niche**: Travel

- **Sub-niche**: Solo travel for women
- **Sub-sub-niche**: Women of color

So this may look like, "I help women of color learn how to travel solo."

Keep in mind; you don't want to niche down so deep that you are only talking to a handful of people.

Positioning

Let's talk about positioning.

Definition: "How you differentiate your product or service from that of your competitors and then determine which market niche to fill."

You must be able to articulate how your brand sets itself apart from similar brands in the industry. Additionally, you must continue to make sure these differences and features are apparent to your audience. How you position yourself and your brand is everything.

Let's use one of my favorite examples: Bottled water.

Look at the following three bottled water brands:
- Fiji
- SmartWater
- Generic Natural spring water from the gas station

While all of these products are the same - water packaged into a bottle-each product is seen very differently to the consumer.

Fiji is the water that is seen as exotic and exclusive because the water is sourced from a waterfall in the South Pacific. Whether or not this is true, Fiji is at a higher price point, has unique packaging, and those who are willing to spend more money on this experience - will.

SmartWater has positioned themselves as a solution for those that are health conscious and desire an option outside of sports drinks. This brand differentiates themselves by claiming features such as electrolytes enhanced and vapor distilled.

Then there's my favorite - regular 'ol generic brand, bottled water. You know, the cheap brand you get from the gas station. There aren't many features except that it is likely the most inexpensive option.

All three brands had the SAME product but positioned in three completely different ways that target very different people.

As a Travel Influencer, especially, someone who is a new Influencer, how are you positioning your brand?

You must be very specific. Think about what is innovative about your brand. What can you offer that no one else can?

Here Are Four Steps to Take When Positioning Your Brand:

1) **Determine How Your Brand is Positioned**: Ask five people who have seen your brand/ social media and ask them how they perceive it. If you haven't started yet - that's cool. Discuss the idea of your brand to a few trusted people and see how they would categorize your brand in the industry.

2) **Research and Define Your Competitors**: Now, I hate the word "competition," but in this case, you want to find those who have a similar brand to yours.

Look and see:
- What are they offering?
- What makes them unique?
- What type of content is delivering? How much? How long?

Take inventory.
Analyze your positioning to your competitors to identify your uniqueness.

3) **Create a Distinct and Value-based Positioning Statement**: At this point, you will have a clearer idea of what your brand is, what it is not, and who you are serving. A value-based positioning statement is an internal guide that dictates the marketing of your business. A positioning statement helps you make decisions that affect how customers perceive your brand.

How To Create A Brand Positioning Statement:

Consider these four crucial elements when creating your Positioning Statements.
1) **What Is My Market Definition?:** What category is your brand competing in and in what context does your brand resonate with your customers?
2) **Who Is Your Target Audience**: What are the demographics and psychographics of the target group for your brand? What is attempting to appeal to and attract them to you?
3) **Brand Promise**: What is the most compelling (emotional/rational) benefit to your target audience that your brand can own relative to your competition?
4) **Reason to Believe**: What evidence do you have or can provide that your brand will deliver on its brand promise?

HACK: Use This Formula When Creating Your Brand Positioning Statement:

[Brand Name] enables/helps [target audience] to experience/ have/ understand [market definition] that delivers/because [brand promise] because/and [reason to believe].

Here Is An Example: [Tony's Travel Tribe] helps [American, Millennial, men of color] understand [how to become an expat successfully] because [we have been living abroad for three years] and [understand and know the benefits of living abroad].

4) Develop Your Brand 'tone': How will you sound?

When I first started RachelTravels.com, I spoke very formally and corporate. I had just left my corporate job and was still in the mode of sending official emails and proposals. Then, I decided to sound like me! Including writing in my Southern accent and throwing in a few "choice" words. This allowed my audience to see me as a "human" and less of a personal brand.

Why There Is No Such Thing As "Competition":

One of my favorite quotes by yours truly is, "There are over 7 billion people in this world. There is more than enough for everybody!".

Even if you had all of the resources, funding, tools, labor, help, and anything else you think you need, you still would not be able to reach or service everyone in the world.
And you wouldn't want to! Who wants that type of pressure anyway?!

TRUTH BOMB: Everyone will not like you. Everyone will not resonate with you.

And that's okay. It's fantastic!

There is this theory in the business world that, "you only need 1000 fans". Fans are people who love and support you. And if you can get those 1000 fans to buy from you – well, you do the math. When you tell your Story, those who 'get it' will be magnetized to you.

And ultimately, desire what you have to offer.

It's that simple.

Many will debate this, but "competition" is a psychological hang-up. In this very abundant Universe, there is enough for everybody.

The best thing to do is create goals and laser focus on them.

Stay In Your Lane

You have probably heard the term, "stay in your lane."

One of the most iconic visual and literal examples of "staying in your lane" is from the 2016 Olympics with Michael Phelps and Chad Le Clos. Chad Le Clos, Brazil's top swimmer, and Michael Phelps, the worlds greatest swimmer of all time, are competing for the Gold Medal in the 200M Butterfly. In the last stretch of the swimming lap, Le Clos looks over into Phelps lane, while Phelps is laser-focused on the finish line. Phelps wins the competition while Le Clos is defeated, yet again. There is an iconic photo showing how that very second of looking over into Phelp's lane, distracted Le Clos, causing him to lose the Gold medal in the race.

Concerns and Misconceptions About 'Competition'

"The Market Is Oversaturated": Some misconceptions or concerns out there about picking a niche are that the market is too oversaturated. Honestly, if there are already Brands out there doing what you are doing or desire to do- this is a great thing! It means that people are already interested in a product or service and you don't have to re-create the wheel. And you have other brands you can study and learn from their strategies.

Have you been down the bread aisle in the grocery store lately? Exactly.

"I Don't Know Enough About the Topic": Sometimes we assume that we don't know enough about our particular niche. We likely know more about your subject and niche than the average person.

Try This: If you walk into a grocery store and know more about the subject than 70% of the people in there - you are likely well-versed.

Think about it, if you're a certified scuba diver and walk into your local grocery store, you likely know more about scuba diving than 70% of the people there.

If you still feel unsure, you can read tons of books on your topic and become a real expert in your niche. A good start is ten to fifteen books on one single subject (i.e., scuba diving).

"There Is Already Enough Free Information Out There": "There's so much 'free' information out there, why would anyone want to pay me?".

One thing to remember is, people are not paying for information, and they are paying for ease and convenience.

Sure, there are plenty of free resources out there on how to become a Travel Influencer, but how long will it take you to scrape and piecemeal all of the blogs posts, videos, and websites all over the vast Internet and put it all together?

When first starting my journey, I was worn out and exhausting from trying to "piece-meal" information together that I gathered from free resources online. When I started investing in coaching, courses, and reading material, I was able to shorten the learning curve immensely.

WORKBOOK FOR FINDING YOUR NICHE:

Instructions: Fill out the questions below to determine what the niche of your brand.

QUESTION: Will this niche hold your interest?

(Yes/No) _____

Is your niche something that will hold your interest for at least 2-3 years? Of course the goal is to make money, but is this niche something that will also keep you excited for that time frame?

QUESTION: Is there pain and/or urgency in this niche?

(Yes/No) _____

Niches where there is pain, urgency, and FOMO (fear of missing out) tend to be the most popular and have high profit potential.

QUESTION: Is there free information in your niche?

(Yes/No) _____

If there is free information in your niche, that's a good thing. In many circumstances, the more free information and free solutions there are, the better. The more free information there is, generally, the harder it is to find good, clear, concise, organized, high quality information on that subject. That's a good thing because people are willing to pay to have those attributes.

QUESTION: Are people asking questions in your niche? (Yes/No)

_____

Look at large communities online (Facebook Groups are a great place to start). Are people asking and answering questions? If yes, this is a great indicator that people are seeking the information.

QUESTION: Is your niche evergreen?

(Yes/No) _____

Evergreen is essentially a topic that will never "expire" and there will always be a demand. If there are always people seeking this information, this means that you will always have a steady flow of new eyes seeking your content and paying for it.

CHAPTER THREE

Storytelling + The Know, Like, & Trust Factor & How to Create and Maintain It

How To Use Your Story to Build Your Brand and Influence:

In this era of "flexin" for the 'Gram (or any social media platforms for that matter), it is hard to sift through what is realistic and attainable and what is fake.

For most of us, it gets difficult to keep up with a persona that is not you. By being authentic and telling your story, sharing your passions, and genuinely being valuable to others - you have no choice but to flourish.

Your audience will resonate with what they can relate to and become invested in your brand.

When first starting RachelTravels.com, I was vanilla vague, and honestly quite dull. I was sharing knowledge, beautiful images, and valuable posts on travel, yet people could not understand how I was able to travel so much, why I decided to travel indefinitely, and what they could also do to obtain the same.

By deciding to lift the veil, I wrote a super vulnerable blog post called, "Why I Left My Good Job." It was this post that moved the needle in my brand, where I spoke very openly about my battle with Anxiety Disorder, Depression, and the comfortable life that I gave up, to create, build, and live the life I wanted to live wholeheartedly.

That particular blog post went viral, and I received a ton of comments from many people who also resonated with battling with mental illness and being unfulfilled.

Not only did this allow me to feel free to build this authentic brand, but I gained respect, credibility, and created a tribe that resonated with my story (and later trusted me enough to purchase my products and services).
Now, this does not mean you have to give every detail of trauma and drama. Share what you're comfortable sharing with the world.

Just make sure it comes from a real place.

Everyone's journey is different.

The point is, tell your story.

What will give your story more of an impact is not to omit the parts where you messed up. Your audience will find wisdom, admiration, and golden nuggets.
Be open. Be honest. Be authentic.

Creating the 'Know, Like, & Trust' Factor

Let's discuss one of the essential elements of becoming a profitable Travel Influencer, and it's creating the "Know, Like, & Trust" factor (KLTF).

We are going to discuss how to get it and how to maintain it.

Through the KLTF, people will start to resonate with you and your brand, where they feel a sense of certainty, confidence, or even faith. Your audience senses that what you say or do is truthful, authentic, and real.

Like any relationship, it builds in phases.

Your audience will start to get to "know" you. In the beginning stages, you'll be sharing lots of valuable content. They will begin to warm up to you, your content, and your presence. Hence, why it is vitally important to be consistent.

Then, over time your audience will start to "like" you. Here is where, like in a relationship; you 'catch feelings.'

Lastly, they begin to trust you.

As a Travel Influencer, trust looks like:
- Your audience asking for your thoughts and insights
- Them commenting that they made a decision based off of your content and value you provided
- Them purchasing your products and services.

Let's take at Oprah as a significant influencer.

She has the ultimate KLTF.

Using her book club as an example, when Oprah mentions that she read a book and gives it her stamp of approval, then the author's career soars to new heights. People who may have never read for leisure or not that particular genre will rush to bookstores to grab their copy, just because Oprah recommended it. Thus, sending the author in the "Bestseller's List."

It was Oprah's stamp of approval that people knew, liked, and trusted.

As a Travel Influencer, your goal is to create the KLTF.

As a profitable Travel Influencer, the goal is to create your KLTF as quickly as possible so you can get to generate reoccurring sales.

Now, you're probably wondering how do you build the KLTF quickly and maintain it. At the end of this chapter, you will find strategies to implement immediately.
However, you must always remember to be valuable, actionable, and consistent.

Consistency is everything.

Consistency is how you will see growth and your momentum taking off.

It is important to point out that as we are striving to become profitable Travel Influencers. It takes a person a minimum of seven times, to see you and read and consume your content before they consider purchasing from you.

As you become more consistent building the KLTF, when launching a product or service, you see the money roll in and not the dreaded sound of crickets. We will get into making sales later on in the book.

Ultimately, you want people to stop and think, " Wow! If their free content is this good and valuable, then I can only imagine that the paid content is even better!"

Ten Strategies to Start Implementing to Build Your 'Know, Like, & Trust' Factor:

- **Develop a Valuable Free Product**: You may hear it called a "lead magnet," "freebie," "opt-in" and more names. However, this is primarily a free, super valuable 'thing' that you offer your audience in exchange for their email. Also, an excellent way to build your email list. One of my first free offers was a PDF called "The 90 Second Guide To Cheap Travel". This helped establish me as a trusted brand who knew how to travel inexpensively and grew my email list so I can stay in touch with people who were interested in learning how to travel economically.

- **Guest Post/ Appear On Other Platforms**: You want as many people to see and hear your expertise as possible. Consider writing a guest post on another blog that is similar to yours or appearing on video, podcast, or another channel, as a guest for someone. A strategy which is one of the quickest and easiest ways to spread your brand awareness and allows you to get in front of new people who may share similar interests. As a resource, there's a post on RachelTravels.com called, "The Easy Way to Get Featured in 100s of Publications".

- **Be Visible**: This may be difficult for some because many people tend to be camera shy. While posting online content is great, if you want to create the KLTF, you want to show up on video! There are so many platforms to choose from, so pick your favorite and drop a video once a week (at least). When doing this, I always see an increase in my online sales.

- **Initiate Conversations**: Ask your audience to engage and interact with you. Pose questions, respond to all their comments on social media and ask them to participate with you.

- **Be Relevant**: This is quite simple, but many people are not always relevant when it comes to building their brand. It's important to listen, research, and ask questions to discover your audience's triggers, fears, and concerns. From here, you can package your ideas into blog posts, video episodes, webinars, or even an email.

- **Create Something Weekly**: Create something that you put out once a week, including video, tips, hacks, or a post. In the early stages of building the KLTF, it's important to give your audience something to look forward to seeing or hearing from you and your brand.

- **Position Yourself As The Expert in Your Niche**: Use your super valuable content to position yourself as an authority in your niche. Back up what you have to say with solid examples, case studies, testimonials, and other evidence (if you have it), as this will solidify you as the 'go to' person about your topic.

- **Ask Your Audience To Share**: You will be surprised. When you ask people to do something, they typically do it. Use this to your advantage. When posting content, ask your followers to share it with others who would find it useful as well

- **Create 'Challenges' or Webinars**: These are, by far, some of the fastest ways to build your KLTF. Create a '5-day challenge' and ask your audience to opt-in and invite their friends. Another way is to create a free webinar/ live class and share actionable and valuable steps for them to take to achieve a particular result.

- **Be Authentic**: This goes without saying.

CHAPTER FOUR

Branding + Website

What Is Branding?

Usually, when people think of building a brand, they assume it is how the brand looks aesthetically.

While this is very important, branding is more than just your website colors, logos fonts, and look. Your brand is a reflection of who you are and the experience you want to create when people interact with it.

What is important is the feelings and emotion that you put into creating your brand. When you are passionate about what you do and authentic in whom you are, you will attract your tribe and inspire others.

Let's be clear; aesthetics are paramount when building your brand and website.

When you begin to think about the aesthetic of your brand consider the following:

- **Research "color psychology":** This is a fascinating study on how colors and hues can affect the mood and psyche of the human mind. There is a reason that most cereal brands use bright colors like reds and oranges.
- **Pick Your Signature Colors:** Based on what you learned with color psychology, choose two or three colors that pop, as your signature colors for your brand.

- **Choose Fonts:** Pick only two fonts for your brand. One should be a regular font and the other a script (cursive- like).

A great way to get inspiration is to look up "mood boards." You can even hire a designer that can create custom mood boards based on what you want your audience to see and feel from your brand.

Most importantly, make sure that you keep the same brand colors, fonts, and aesthetic everywhere your brand appears (social media, website, webinars, PDFs, etc.).

You will never see your favorite brand use a different logo, fonts, and colors across various media platforms.

*Note: Please do not spend a TON of time on this. Many people have been putting off building empires because they're stuck on colors and fonts.

Elements You Need For a Profitable Website

No matter how you show up online, you must have a website. A website and a blog are not synonymous. A site is your slice of the online real estate where people can learn more about you, the brand, contact you, and is a 24-hour sales team. Consider this "home base."

While every website is different, you want to make sure that your site includes these essential elements. The "elements" listed below are links you should have at the top of your navigation menu of the website, so people will come to your site always have an option to click it. They are:

HOME PAGE: This is a given; however, you want people to be able to navigate back 'Home' where they have options to go to other areas on your site.

ABOUT ME/US: Did you know that the 'About Me/Us' page is the second most visited page on your site? People need to know who you are and why your brand was created. Use this to tell your audience about yourself, mention top content, and introduce your products and services.

SHOP: If your goal is to become a profitable Travel Influencer, then you want people to navigate to your products/ services quickly so that they can make quick (er) purchasing decisions.

BLOG (or content): Whether you are blogging, have a video channel, or podcast, there must be a link where people can navigate to all your excellent content.

RESOURCE/ FREEBIE: You should be offering some free incentive(s) in exchange for emails. Create an entire page dedicated to this, to convince people to opt-in and join your email list. For example, I committed a full page to my Media Kit Template freebie. We will go more into Email Marketing later in the book.

SOCIAL MEDIA: Make sure links navigate directly to your social media handles.

CONTACT: You want to make it easy for people to get in touch with you, especially when you start working with brand partners and sponsors.

Choosing A Domain Name + Hosting:

Domain Names:

Without being too complicated, it is vital that you make sure when creating your site, that your domain name is the same as your brand name, or, get it as close as possible. It is essential to ensure that your domain name (or website name) is easily recallable. Anything too long, complicated, or hard to spell, will make it difficult for people to search or remember.

If you can, choose a domain with .com, at the end.

Hosting:

Once you have purchased your domain, you will need to "host" your website.

Think of a domain as the "house" on the real estate market, but you need "land" to place your house.

There are plenty of online companies that can offer to host for relatively inexpensively.

There are even services that include the website designs, hosting, and domain in one packaged service for a flat rate or monthly fee.

How To Create An Interesting 'About Me/Us' Page

As mentioned, your 'About Me' page is the second most visited page after the Homepage. Your 'About Me/Us' page should convey:

- Who you are
- What you are doing
- How you are serving
- How you got there

And although it is an 'About Me/Us' page, you want to explain how what you are creating is about them (your audience).

The Goal Of The 'About Me/Us' Page Is To;
- Grab the reader's' attention
- Provide you with a level of credibility
- Make you relatable
- Convey how you are valuable to your target audience
- Be unforgettable
- Convert readers into fans, subscribers, and customers

Note: I've changed my "About Me" page a gazillion times. Don't get stuck on this.

How To Write A Captivating "About Me/ Us" Page

If you want to write a dope 'About Me' page, follow the following criteria:

Begin With a Great and Captivating Headline: You only have about five to seven seconds to grab your reader's attention. Make sure your headline starts strong to hook the reader so that they can continue to read and learn more about you.

Be Clear About Who You Are Servicing: Make it very clear who your target audience is and how you help them. This is how you can eliminate those who otherwise would not have an interest in your content. Here's an example, "I help millennial women of color learn how to transition and navigate living abroad." If you are a person who does not immediately identify with this, then they likely will not continue to roam around your site – which is precisely what you want.

Share About Yourself: As mentioned, it is essential to building the KLTF. Be open and vulnerable here. Share your 'why.' While it does not always have to be something drastic and life-altering, share the moment when you decided to create your brand to serve others. Share some of those cool, funny, relatable aspects of your life. This will humanize your brand.

Visuals: Make sure to include images of you doing what you do (concerning your brand). You want people to resonate with you. Displaying bright, fun, and clear photos are a great way to do that. Many people are visual learners, so by showing imagery, you create a level of social proof.

Credibility + Expertise: This is where you can share testimonials, compliments, and other proof that you are legit. However, if you are starting and do not have any credibility yet, then share personal experiences, past achievements, etc. Doing this will help the reader better see you as a credible source in your niche.

Offer Value: At the end of your 'About Me' page, you should offer something valuable, like your free incentive/option/freebie/ lead magnet in exchange for an email. You want them to stay connected, continue to come back, and continue to build that rapport with them.

Contact: Make it easy to communicate with you by integrating a Contact Form.

CHAPTER FIVE

Content Creation

To demystify what it means to be a "Travel Influencer" let us first clear the notion that you must be a blogger. Not true. Content can show up in many forms including:

- **Written**: Blogging, books, essays, white papers, etc.
- **Audio**: Podcasts, radio shows, audio lessons, etc.
- **Visuals**: Graphics, images, infographics, etc.
- **Video**: Live streaming, video channels, vlogging, etc.

"Content is queen (or king)."

No matter which type of content you decide to create, it must be valuable.

Keyword: Valuable.   The goal is for people to walk away from your content feeling: educated, motivated, or inspired.

Transparency Moment! The first posts on RachelTravels.com were super corny and boring! There were posts about my favorite travel apps, rambles about topics not about travel, and other random foolishness. Snooze-fest!

Perhaps it is useful to some but not nearly as useful as valuable as the post on, "How I Spent $126 in Bogota, Colombia."

See the difference there?

Think quality versus quantity.

It is easy to assume that having a lot of content is better than having less.

Writing five, valuable, actionable blog posts is much more relevant than having twenty blog posts that are full of vague information, have no real context, nor provide actionable steps.

The audience is not seeking to read bite-sized pieces of 'stuff.' The amount of content you have is irrelevant if people are not reading it, inspired by it, or isn't sharing it.

Your time is valuable and so is your brand. Allow the quality content you create to be a reflection of that.

How Are You Showing Up?

Listen.

If you genuinely do not enjoy writing or will not be consistent with it, then do not become a blogger! Simple.

You must pick the way that is most comfortable for you AND where you can get the most engagement from your audience.

TIP: Create The Type Of Content That Will Move the Needle
Creating content via videos is very powerful. It is also the quickest way to grow your KLTF, gain momentum for your brand, and the method that gets the highest amount of engagement.

Many people feel uncomfortable with being on camera, but creating a profitable online brand (or any venture) is going to push you to some uncomfortable limits.

If creating a video is uncomfortable, try practicing by speaking in the mirror. Talk as if you are chatting with your friends.

You can even pre-record videos.

Once you become comfortable, move toward leveraging live streaming.

You will find what works and what sticks with your audience sooner than you realize.

Once you have created content, make sure that people continually see the content by optimizing how much it shows up. There is tons of great software on the market that will allow you to make your content Evergreen (content that will never get "old"; it is always relevant).

We will discuss automating and optimizing content later in the book.

Lastly, through the process of creating content (and various types), you will begin to clearly understand what kind of material will best resonate with your audience by the amount of traffic, comments, or engagement. This may take some time to figure out, but you will have to test, test, test, and see.

Here Are a Few Ways to Measure This:

• Do you have high engagement when you do live video online? If so, this suggests that people are highly engaged and excited when you do live video.
• Is your email open rates high? This indicates that people enjoy reading emails from you.
• Do you get a considerable amount of likes and comments on your social media posts?
• Have you created an exclusive community and received a lot of engagement in your group without much work from you? This suggests that people like the idea of an 'exclusive' community and you are showing up there to support them.

Search Engine Optimization (SEO):

Search Engine Optimization (SEO) is defined as the process of how your content is found through unpaid search results. Similarly, this is often referred to as "organic" traffic or results.
The idea is that you want to create content that will appear in online search results at the top or within the first three pages.

There is a lot that goes into SEO, so I challenge you to study more about the subject. However, utilizing the right keywords and understanding how search engines work is what you should be an area of focus.

One of the best ways to get started with SEO is to create creative, catchy headlines for all of your content.

HACK: Use Catchy Headlines to Get People to Read Your Content.

One of the essential elements of content creation is coming up with catchy titles. You want people to read the title and be eager to consume the rest of the content.

Here are five tips for creating catchy headlines:
- **Use Specific Data and Numbers**: "How To Spend $50/day in Cuba."

- **Create a Sense of Urgency**: "How to Beat the Social Media Algorithm Before Everyone Figures It Out."

- **Educate**: Starting with "How To" is a great way to educate and create actionable content, "How To Travel Hack Flights."

- **Use Verbiage That Stirs Up Emotions**: Great keywords to use are; essential, absolute, effortless, and incredible. Example: "The Effortless Way to Get International Flights For Under $500".

- **Start With A Question**: "Tired of paying too much for flights? Here are four travel hacking tips!"

Why Social Media Is Not Discussed In This Book:

Social media is always changing.

The algorithms associated with social media platforms are always changing. Learning about social media, how to gain followers, how to optimize your content, and get seen will be continual learning because it is ever changing.

Because of this, I decided to omit strategies to grow your social media on specific platforms. Since writing this book, the algorithm has changed twice on a particular social media platform.

Do you remember MySpace? Vine?

All were prevalent social media platforms that are no longer with us.

My recommendation is to choose two platforms and study it through and through.

Understand and learn who are the primary users of the platforms.
• Which functionalities does your audience engage with the most (images, videos, "stories," live video)
• Understand how the platform works.
• Research the best practices and ways to grow on that account
Above all, you guessed it – be consistent!

How to Create Content If You're Not Traveling:

A considerable concern people have when they are looking to be a Travel Influencer is how to create content even when they're not traveling.

There are several ways that you can curate content. Here are three different methods:

A) Turn One Experience Into Several Types Of Content

The way that you can create content if you are not traveling or will not be traveling is to take an experience and break it down into several parts, which you can then build out multiple pieces of content.

Let's take Thailand for example. Say you went to Thailand last year with a group of your girlfriends.

You can take this one experience and break it down into five different types of content. Here are the examples:

#1: How To Plan A Girls' Trip To Thailand:

You can talk about what it takes to coordinate a group of friends to go to Thailand. Include how to find accommodations, things to do, how you would break down costs, how to decide what everyone wants to do, and even mention how to create synergy amongst the different personalities within the group.

You could even create a sample itinerary.

#2: Do A Hotel Review:

You could do a full analysis and a hotel review. If you choose to do a hotel review, take it a bit further and reach out to the hotel and pitch them on the idea. Perhaps if your brand is still new, an agreement may not be monetary but could look like a complimentary night's stay, a spa treatment, or dinner.

#3: Top X Things to Try In Thailand:

Pretty straightforward. If there were some experiences that you highly recommend to those who would like to visit

Thailand, then create content about this very topic. You can discuss the attractions they should see or even reveal some secret bars that you should experience while there.

#4: Top X Things To Eat In Thailand:

If you're a foodie and food is a huge part of how you experience travel, then mention some of the best meals that one must try when visiting, along with any particular restaurants or eateries.

#5: Scams To Watch Out For/ Safety Tips While in Thailand:

No matter where you travel in the world, if it is a high tourist area, then scams are likely to occur. If there are some hacks on how to stay safe and healthy, as well as insight you can share on what to watch out for a while traveling, then you can create content as a solution to these concerns.

There are countless other topics and ideas you can cover from your experience. Be creative, make it actionable, and have fun!

B) Become A Tourist in Your Backyard

There is an opportunity for you to stretch your muscle when it comes to pitching brands.

Create content by exploring and discovering more in your city.

Reach out to new restaurants, bars or hotels that have recently opened up or getting ready to launch.

Pitch them on creating a review as an exchange or ask to be paid to develop marketing materials for them to use.

You can also create content about cool things to see and do in your city. Perhaps you know about spots that only the locals know, love, and patronize. Share that with your audience.

You can also talk about some of the food in your city or your city's history.

The topics were endless!

C) Helpful Travel Tips

When you're not traveling, consider creating content on preparing for travel.

If you are a solo traveler, what are some things that you put in place before traveling? What are some of your favorite essentials that you pack?

Think about all of those aspects that you can start creating. What are some of the things that you do?

Get creative. There are a lot of things that you can do.

How To Be Consistently Consistent

As you have been reading this book, a consistent theme is the importance of being consistently consistent. If you genuinely want to be a Travel Influencer, especially one that has made the business of influence profitable, you must be consistent in how you show up and in what you produce.

Yes, it is true - life happens. So, being consistently consistent can be difficult at times. However, having a strategy and plan in place can help you position yourself to be consistent without being overwhelmed and without putting a ton of pressure on yourself.

Remember consistency is essential to remember that to build the KLTF.

Here are some suggestions to achieve this:

#1: Set Goals For Yourself And Brand

Create goals and intentions for what you want to make.

If this looks like growing your following on social media, then come up with a strategy that will allow you to be consistent with a growth strategy.
If it looks like publishing content once a week, then write out an outline for each piece of material and tackle it from there.

Setting goals and holding yourself (or asking someone) to hold you accountable is a great way to be consistent.

#2: Batch Your Content

One of the ways to be consistently consistent is to batch your content. You will be doing the work up front. One suggestion is to work a month in advance. I've been creating content like this for years.

Start by creating a month's worth of content, then schedule it out for the following month. The month before, prepare the rough drafts, edit and revise - whatever you need to do to make and schedule it a month ahead.

The same goes for social media. There are so many programs, tools, and software out there where you can schedule posts, images, captions, and hashtags. From here, it will automatically post for you, or you may get a notification to publish the content to the platform manually.

This way, you can still "show up" and be consistent without continually having to write content or create content, in real time.

#3: Pick A Date And Time Weekly To Dedicate Time To Working On Your Brand

Pick a time and a date every week, or even every day, where you lock in and dedicate time to work on your brand. This will begin to create a routine and a habit of working diligently on building your brand.

Quick Challenge: Decide on a day and time to dedicate to working on your brand, "Every Tuesday at 7.30 pm; I will go live on a topic or a travel tip." Set the reminder(s) in your calendar.

Before doing this, make sure you have prepared by creating a list of ten to thirty topics to discuss, this way, when it's time for you to go live, you're not scrambling trying to figure out what you want to discuss.

PRO TIP: Project Management Software

If you are super organized or prefer constant reminders, then consider using project management software. There are many free online project management software out there. You can create 'projects,' then add various tasks, like writing your posts, getting them edited, filming your videos, getting them published, scheduling social media, and so on. Add deadlines, and the software will send reminders about the tasks you to complete. Using PM software will keep you focused and accountable.

HACK: Recording and Getting Your Work Transcribed

Here is a quick game-changing hack to creating quality, consistent, content quickly. It's actually how I "wrote" this book!

This hack will also help you get through frustration and overwhelm when it comes to creating written content.
Here are the steps:

1. Open the Voice Recorder app on a smartphone.
2. Sit in a quiet area and record the content that you want to have as a blog post or as a caption or a show notes or anything and sit down and press play and record yourself. Record what would have taken time to type out.
3. Save and send the recording to your computer.
4. Go to a site like Fiverr.com or UpWork.com and search for a "Transcriber."
5. After hiring them, send them the audio notes you saved from your smartphone.

Within a few days, they will send you back your audio notes in text form, typically in a Word document.

Your job is to take that text, edit it, add images, links, and the other elements you need - then, boom! You've just "written" something without physically typing it out.

Simple.

The ONE Method That Can Take You From Unnoticed To Poppin':

Do live videos.

When we're starting, many of us feel uncomfortable about doing live video online. Those insecurities start kicking in big time.

We get nervous.
Wonder if we will mess up.
Do we look okay?
Will anyone show up?

Yes, in all honesty, it can be nerve-racking to go live online. There could be potentially hundreds of people watching you and listening to what you have to say.

Do not allow this to intimidate you. Here is your opportunity to position yourself as the expert in your niche.

By doing live video, you will not only move the needle and get outside of your comfort zone, but also build your 'Know, Like, and Trust' factor quickly.

People enjoy connecting with you in real time. They want to hear your voice, see your idiosyncrasies, get real-time advice. Insights from you, and genuinely connect!

Through real connection and consistency, you will quickly go from being unnoticed to poppin'.

So, I challenge you to 'go live'!

Follow this challenge below to help you get out of your comfort zone and begin to move the needle in your business.

CHALLENGE

Objective: Get comfortable with going live online.

Make sure that when you go live, it is on the platform(s) where your people most likely utilize and will find you. This will take some testing out, but you got this.

Instructions to the Challenge:

1. Pick the platform(s) that you will be going live on.

2. Create a list of ten to twenty ideas to discuss with your audience.

3. Decide how often you will go live over the next thirty days. If you created ten topics, then do live video twice a week. If you create thirty subjects, then do live video daily.

4. Make sure that you choose the same time. You want to 'train' people to know when you'll show up for them so they can be waiting for you.

5. GO LIVE!

Strategies To Help You Promote Your Live Videos:

• Start by building excitement by sharing what you will be talking about on the video. Ex: "I am going live tomorrow night at 7:30 p.m. EST on [insert social media platform], talking about
____."
• Create a visually appealing social media images to get your audience excited.
• Share your social media promotion post across all of the places you show up online.
• Announce that you're going live to your email list.
• During and after ever Live, ask those who show up to invite others and to share the replay.
• Send a follow-up email to your List asking them to watch the replay.

HACK: Hire Help Dammit!

It's inexpensive to hire a Virtual Assistant (VA) who can do the things you don't want to do.

A few examples include:
- Reading and replying to emails
- Pitching brands on your behalf
- Recording an audio message then hiring someone to transcribe it into blog posts
- Editing video
- Creating graphics
- Scheduling your social media
- Pretty much anything.

The earlier you can get someone on your team that can help you in these aspects, the better! This will allow you to not only free up time but gives you the mental capacity to be creative and develop super compelling and valuable content.

How to Get Published in Hundreds of Publications

As you are creating your brand as a Travel Influencer, it is essential to earning some 'street cred.' One of the best and fastest ways to gain momentum and credibility for your brand is to appear in several different online publications, including podcasts, blogs, vlogs, radio shows, and audio broadcasts.

If you're like most of us, then you probably do not have time to research hundreds of blog, podcasts, YouTube channels, radio stations, etc. to pitch your brand to be featured or appear as a guest. This may seem daunting initially, but it is not difficult to get featured in various publications, podcasts, and radio shows.

Before we get into how to get featured, it is imperative that you have already established: solid brand, know your target audience and positioned in a way that is in alignment with those publications where you want to be featured. Now, this also doesn't mean you have to have a large following; it just means you have to have something to show for your brand.

Deeper than this, you must pitch your brand to similar brands where there is alignment.

The way to save yourself a ton of time and effort is to outsource someone to do this for you.

Here is the step-by-step guide on how to do this:

1. Decide what your mission is and what you want to share with people online. Since we are talking about travel, then you want to find brands that discuss travel. But do not stop there, if your brand is about traveling solo, then you want to think about publications that talk about:
    - Solo travel
    - Women, in travel
    - Dating (perhaps what it is like dating abroad)
    - How to travel as a family, as a single parent, co-parenting, etc.

It is essential that you know what your message and brand are, and how you are positioned, so you can handle step #2 with ease.

2. Once you are extremely clear on your brand and have decided what your message is, determine what type of podcasts, publications, and radio shows, etc. will most align with your brand.

As an example, if you are a parent who has excellent parenting hacks for traveling with children, you want to align with other brands that also discuss parenting, organization, lifestyle hacks, productivity hacks, etc.

Assignment: Write a list of three to five topics that you think will most align with your brand.

3. Head over to the Fiverr, UpWork, or other platforms where you can find a virtual assistant (VA).

For steps, #1 and #2, create a document to outline your brand and what types of topics you want to cover.

Pro Tip: If you are on a budget, find a VA that you can pay between $4 - $7 an hour. You can do this by looking for a virtual assistant from the Philippines. They tend to speak the best English and are quite well versed in working online.

4. Create a Standard Operating Procedure (SOP) or a simple Google Doc for your Virtual Assistant.

In the Document, explain:

- What your Brand is, who you serve and what the mission (From Step #1)
- Outline the 3-5 topics you can discuss (From Step #2)
- Create a sample pitch template

5. Have your VA research a minimum of 100 publications (this includes podcasts, blogs, blogs, radio shows, even local shows, etc.) that you put on a spreadsheet.

6. Have your VA send these pitches to the researched publications. Lastly, wait for the responses!

Note: Be VERY detailed. It is crucial that you tell your Virtual Assistant the number of hours that you think it will take them to complete the job.

CHAPTER SIX

Monetizing Your Influence

Let's be honest.

We all would love to get paid or compensated for traveling.

Up until now, this book has focused on how to begin to build your brand, how to create content and other elements for creating an excellent brand.

Due to travel becoming essential to happiness and becoming more accessible to all; many new and inspiring travel bloggers/vloggers/ podcasters/ are looking to get paid and compensated for their influence.

Understand, it takes a lot of hard work, diligence, ignored messages, and consistency to get to a position of working with major brands.

Prepare your mind for this journey.

If you're not going to be committed, then growing any successful brand may not be for you.

Now, this was mentioned earlier in the book; however, it is worth mentioning the following points again. If you truly understand and are very clear about the following, you will be halfway to getting paid and compensated for your influence:

1) **There is no such thing as "free"**: As beautiful as your images may be or the amount of valuable content you produce, no one is going to compensate you based off of this alone. When collaborating and partnering with brands, they will require something from you as you would from them. This could include blog posts, video, reviews on specific sites, etc. There will be work and effort put into this partnership.

2) **You MUST Understand Your Audience & The Brands' Needs**: This is possibly the most important point for you to remember. This sounds like a broken record. But, you must be VERY clear with your audience. If you have no idea of or not sure of exactly who you're talking to, under their needs, desires, etc. it will be difficult to convince a brand that collaborating is mutually beneficial.

3) **This is a Business Transaction**: Seriously. You're not just getting free nights to stay at a beautiful resort and villa. You're waiting to document your experiences, writing about it, creating attractive, aesthetically appealing content, etc. As mentioned in an earlier point, you are getting to give. Furthermore, if you desire to work with other brands, you must take this seriously and with pride. Your name is on it.

4) **Be Different**: Your brand must stand out. Try to understand what the brand is looking for in the Influencers they desire to work with on projects. Ask yourself, how to can be in alignment, but provide a different, exciting, and captivating angle.

How To Make Money From Your Travel Influencer

Learning how to make money online is not that difficult. Understanding what you can offer online that will help you create more clarity on what you can create to sell online.

Here are 10 Ways to Make Income Online as a Travel Influencer:

<u>Digital Products:</u>
• **Guides/ Checklists/ Templates**: Creating PDFs of guides, templates, checklists, etc. is the quickest way to start making money. For sure, this is one of the easiest and fastest ways to make the income - especially on autopilot.
• **Online Courses**: Creating an online course is a bit more involved but a super easy way to make money as a Travel Influencer. There are a few ways to go about creating an online course. You can incorporate software designed for online courses, or you can create your own.

<u>Physical Products:</u>
• **Merchandise**: The one is straightforward. Many people sell t-shirts, travel essentials, bags, and more. If you are looking to bypass researching vendors, shipping, fulfillment, and more complexities, check out dropshipping services that will do the processing and fulfillment for you.

<u>Information:</u>
• **Consulting**: For people who want to "pick your brain," or sit down with you and ask you a ton of questions - create a space to

dedicate time to them. It is as easy as setting up calendar software to schedule appointments and using a live video function like Google Hangouts to speak with them one-on-one. Your time is valuable so make sure you charge for it.

• **Done for You Service**: If you are a Travel Influencer and want to DO or complete a service for someone (i.e., create a website for someone, run their social media, create marketing campaigns, etc.), versus consulting with them, then doing a 'Done-For-You' (DFU), is an excellent option (and lucrative).

Note: This involves more hands-on work on your end, so you want to charge more for this service.

Sponsored Posts + Affiliate Links:
• **Sponsored Posts**: There's a ton of Travel Influencer programs and agencies you can join. You can search online the term, "influencer marketing agencies." Or, Brands may reach out to you. However, sponsored posts are when they send you a product or let you try a service, and you get paid to feature it on your platform.

• **Affiliate Links**: Being an affiliate is getting a commission if someone signs up for a product/ service you suggested. These are links that are assigned a unique code to you, so when anyone clicks on it and signs up, you get a commission for it. A simple example is: Sharing your AirBnB.com code and getting gifting credits for a stay, you then receive a commission in return.

Experiences:
• **Curate Trips**: An excellent way to earn income as a Travel Influencer, is to curate trips to showcase, tour, and experience unique destinations.

• **Home Sharing**: If you have a home with extra space, then you could always put your place on a home-sharing service. Mostly, you rent your own house out to people and make an income from it.

• **Live & Virtual Events**: Creating live events are a tremendous way to earn income as an online Travel Influencer. You can create live, in-person or virtual classrooms educating your audience in your expertise. Promote a topic you want to train your audience on, have them pay to join the live- class, and teach the subject utilizing a system that allows broadcasting video to multiple people.

Understanding Conversion Rates

Often, what happens at the very beginning of building a business is you may not hit your sales goals, followers goals, or traffic goals. Sometimes, when we don't hit our sales goals, we may think there is something wrong with our product, our services, or us. While this could be true, in most cases, it is not and here is the reason why.

There is a science to making sales.

Without getting too complicated, there is an array of formulas, percentages, and rates of conversions.

For now, we will keep it very simple.

If you are selling something via email, let's continue with this example. Say you will send an email to 100 people. Of the thirty percent (30 people) of people who open your email, then it is likely that ten percent (3 of the 30 people) will click on the link. And the rate of purchases is ten percent of that (1 sale).

Do you see how this is a Numbers Game?

While this may sound discouraging, the goal here is to add more, highly targeted people to your email list. Focus on increasing your odds.

Webinars + Live Events:

For live online events or webinars, you can expect that of the number of people that signup, fifty percent of them will show up. Which means if 100 people signed up for your free webinar, then only 50 of them will come on live. If you are pitching a sale toward the end of the live event, then you can expect a ten percent conversion, which means you may be able to make five purchases.

The secret here is to create a sense of urgency and send several follow-up emails reminding them of the thing you have for sale.

Do not take it personally if you are not making the sales that you think you should be making. Once you understand the math, build your audience, and create momentum, you will see an increase in sales.

You are capable of doing this – it takes times, consistency, and dedication.

How to Create Digital Products & Services to Sell in 48 Hours in 6 Simple Steps

Step #1: Validate the Idea

Make sure that people WANT what you are creating! Ask your audience, "If I created _____, would you be interested?"

Ways to Ask:
- Instagram Stories Poll
- Email List
- Facebook
- Wherever YOUR people are online

Step #2: Create Anticipation!
If they are interested, then you need to begin to create anticipation, curiosity, and excitement. This is a GREAT strategy that works well!

Set up a Waiting List (using the email system you chose) and drive people to that list.

This will do three (3) things:
- Create an exclusive, experience.
- Validate even further that people desire the product or service (when people are signing up for it)
- Gives you a working list to sale to when the product is ready to launch

Step #3: Build Your Audience With Free Content
Create a free piece of content to drive people to:
1) Waiting List
2) Digital Product (after launch)

Ways To Promote and Drive People To Your Free Content:
- Blog Posts
- Going Live
- Stories/ Videos
- Podcasts
- Social Media Posts

Step #4: Create The Digital Product

Once steps #1-3 have been done, and people are signing up for your Waiting List, then you want to start creating your digital product.

You can create a digital product in less than 48 hours.

Step #5: Payment Gateways

To start making income online, you have to have a way to receive payments. Make sure you have the RIGHT payment Gateways in place. You can quickly sign up for a free PayPal or Stripe account. However, seek a system that allows you to take payments and tracks analytics.

Step #6: Place Free Content and Paid Product on Autopilot

To create passive income, an EASY way to do this is to put your content on a system that will send it out on autopilot. There are many systems on the market that allows you to upload blog posts, videos, products, and services to your social media platforms. Then, it posts them over and over again at the times and days you have scheduled.

Look For Systems That Offer Great Functionalities Like:
Weekly Analytics: You want to see how your content is performing and which times and days get the most engagement

Scheduling Out The Content: Certain content performs better or worst on certain days and time. Once you have studied your analytics, you can schedule or re-schedule the material on the best days and times that get the most engagement.

How To Figure Out Price Points For Your Products or Services

There are many theories on how to accurately price your products/ services. It comes down to mindset, worth, and the value of your product or service.

Looking at buyer psychology, ending prices in a "7" or "9", works well for selling online, look at your local grocery store prices as an example.

For small digital products and if you are starting, the best rang is between $7- $97, to start.

Here are a few examples:
- TEMPLATE: Travel Budget Template - $7
- TRAVEL GUIDE: "How To Travel To Thailand" - $27
- COURSE: "How To Book An Flight On Google Flights Like A Pro" - $97

As you begin to build your credibility and audience, you can charge more for courses, consulting, and other products/ services.

Why You Need An Email List

One of the things that are essential in starting at the beginning of building a brand as a Travel Influencer, is creating an email list. While it is never too late to start making an email list, it is advised to start as early as possible.

Here are the essential benefits for starting an email list:

• **It Gives Your Access To Your Tribe**: If social media went away tomorrow, then you would have lost your audience. Now, if you had their email addresses, you could still communicate with through newsletter blasts and campaigns.

• **Further Nurture Your KLTF**: Through an email list, you can continue to create and nurture the 'Know, Life, & Trust Factor' (KLTF) by sending valuable an exclusive content, like giving your List first dibs on when you create new content, announcements, and even make them feel like VIP by giving them exclusive offers.

• **Grow Your Following**: The best type of growth is through word-of-mouth. Seriously, if you ask those on your Email List to share something, you will have an overwhelming amount of support.

• **Segment Your Audience**: You can create tailored-made messages for your audience, by segmenting them for their interests. An example of segmenting your email list is to have a separate group of people that you send emails to that want to know about have to travel on a budget. Then, you can have another list that is focusing on hacks for traveling with a family.

• **Feedback + Insights**: Email is an easy way to gain feedback, insights, and opinions from your audience. Because email subscribers trust you enough to give their email, they are more likely to buy your product/ services. More subscribers to your email lists = broader brand awareness and MORE sales!

• **Easy Touch Point**: Email is the easiest way to stay in touch with your audience!

PRO TIP: To be effective in sales, your audience needs to see you 7x before they feel comfortable enough to purchase from you. Use your Email List to your advantage!

How To Build An Email List

To begin to build an email list, you will need to do the following:

1) **Signup for An Email List Program**: You want to find a software service that is easy to get started with (especially if you are not techy).

2) **Grow Your Email List**: There are several ways to increase your email list. Here are three that work great:

   a. **Give Away a Free Piece of Content**: Examples include PDFs, templates, checklists, ebooks, etc. Create signup for in your Email List program and have it automatically send your freebie through automation.

   b. **Run a Contest or Giveaway**: Have potential leads exchange their email addresses to be entered in a giveaway.

   c. **Create a free, exclusive online community**: Ask people who want to join your free community to exchange their emails for entrance into the community. Facebook Groups work exceptionally well with this method.

3) **Start A Challenge**: Starting a challenge is a great way to build out your Email List. Make an announcement for your Challenge and get people to signup before the Challenge starts!

Optimization

Optimize your website and social media with links to enter your email list. Creating "sign up forms" from the email software that you chose in step #1, is how you will do this. This will ensure that those who signup will get the freebie.

You want to engage and captivate your audience. One of the best, most accessible, and a hands-off way to do this is by creating an automated message.

The way it works is, once people have signed up for your email list, the system you use will automatically send a message to the subscriber.
The feature is called an Autoresponder.

Here is a Quick Sample Automated Email Message:

Hey [First Name]!

Thank you for joining my email list!
I'm [Insert Your Name Here] and I am the _____ of [Name of Your Brand].
My brand focuses on [insert 1-3 sentences about what you do and why].

>> Click here to get [the free thing] I promised you.

Before we go, tell me: "What are you struggling with right now?"
Even if it is something small, I'd love to hear more.
Reply and let me know!
Later,

[Insert Your Name]

The point of this email is to:
1) Introduce yourself to the new subscriber.
2) Remind them about the freebie
3) And understand their pain points so you can gather insights and create a solution

Email Open Rates:

According to industry rates, if you have over a 30% open rate (the percentage of people who open your emails), then that is exceptional. What this means is, that for every 100 people that you send an email newsletter to, thirty people open it.

It will take practice to get master Email Marketing. I recommend studying copywriting, best times to send emails for your List, how to segment your List, and so on.

Metrics & Analytics

Analytics and metrics can be a sticky subject. It is vital that you understand how to measure success and what is working and not working for your brand.

Often, we are concerned about the wrong things when it comes to measuring the performance of our brand and most importantly sales.

There are hundreds of tools and functionalities in various software, which allows you to "measure" and analyze various aspects of your business.

For starters, everyone needs to have Google Analytics. You want to connect your GA to your website, which will allow you to manage traffic, clicks, and sales. If you are intimidated by the idea of "metrics," you can hire someone on Fiverr.com for $5 to set up your Google Analytics, walk you through it, and create custom reports that are easy to read and comprehend.

Metrics You Want to Pay Attention To Are:

- **Traffic Sources**: Where did your site visitors come from? What state, country, region? Was it organic search? Social media? Paid Ads?

- **Page Views**: You want to understand which pages on your site are getting the most attention and for how long. This can tell you the type of content your visitors are most interested in seeing; this way, you can create more similar content or schedule it out to be seen more often.

- **Returning Visitors**: Understanding the number of return visitors you have and what they are coming here for is extremely important. This allows you to see that your content is valuable, insightful, and inspiring enough for visitors to return. Once you dive deeper and understand your analytics, you can learn why they are coming back.

You also want to turn on and understand the analytics for the social media platforms you will be utilized most often. You want to track:

- Demographics
- Social Shares
- Link Clicks To Your Other Content Best Times to Post
- What Type of Content Gets the Most Engagement

Metrics and analytics isn't exactly the sexiest topic. Once you nail down the type of content that gets people running back for more, you can optimize what you have and what you will create that keeps them coming back. Ultimately, allowing you to even gain more sales on autopilot when you get to that point.

CHAPTER SEVEN

How to Make Brands Fall In Love With You

A huge aspect of being a Travel Influencer is working with brands and companies – large or small. However, there are characteristics that brands are specifically looking for in Travel Influencers.

Through extensive experience working with various brands in the travel and tourism space, there has been an ongoing trend for what they are looking for in partnerships and collaborations with Influencers.

Here Are Three Points To Consider:

#1: Position Yourself to Be Unique:

Earlier in the book, we covered why there are no such things as competition, but let's be clear, there is such a thing as being vague, watered down, and getting lost in the shuffle because your brand is not unique.

We have gone over this repeatedly in the book, but this is a strong point to understand and comprehend. Ask yourself, "How is my brand different and unique from the other ten Travel Influencers with the same amount of followers and similar content?"

If you cannot answer this clearly and confidently, then you may want to go back to Chapter 2, on building your target audience.

#2: Be Consistently Consistent

I know you're tired of reading this; however, you must embrace this to your core.

Consistency is the key.

If a brand or company does not see you being consistent with your content creation and production, then they will not trust you to create regular, quality content for them either.

#3 Alignment

Brands are looking to work with Travel Influencers who closely align with not only their target audience but to the mission and vision of the company.

Think of it as dating. You want to match up with someone (or a brand) that has similar values and goals as you.

Why You Don't Need a Large Following

Let's demystify one of the most significant concerns and myths about being a profitable Travel Influencer.

Having a large following online does not make or break your brand.

You do not have to have a large following before you start working with brands. What brands and agencies are primarily looking for in Travel Influencers, is a high level of engagement that coincides with the audience that you already have.

Do not allow the number of followers to discourage you.

Let's break this down a bit.

It is no secret that you can purchase followers, comments, and likes.

Don't be fooled. Brands know this and utilize tools and software that run your social media handles, and analyze the authenticity of your followers.

As long as you are uniquely positioned and focused on creating the KLTF with your audience through genuine engagement, brands consider this.

On my first paid sponsored post, I did not have a ton of traffic to my blog. There were less than 600 followers me on social media. Still, the hotel I partnered with saw the value of my content and that the few followers I had were really into what I was producing.

Focus on creating a strong brand, an engaged audience, and having alignment with the companies you desire to partner in the future.

That is the formula for brands to fall in love with you.

The next step is learning the most effective ways to pitch your brand as a Travel Influencer, for partnerships and collaborations; which we will cover in the next chapter.

CHAPTER EIGHT

How To Effectively Pitch Brands

Learning how to pitch brands for collaborations and partnerships effectively is critical. Most people get this part wrong and go completely unnoticed.

The goal of this chapter is to set you up for success in landing your first partnerships with brands! Because who doesn't want to get paid/ compensated for working with brands?

How to Create An Engaging Media Kit:

Before pitching brands, you must create a media kit or press kit, (they are interchangeable).
→ You can grab a free Media Kit Template here:
https://www.racheltravels.com/media-kit-template

A **media kit** is a promotional public relations tool that can serve several functions, including:

- Promoting the launch of a new company

Supporting the launch of a new product or service by an existing company

- Giving a company a way to present itself as it would like to be seen, and/or saving time, by eliminating the need for a company's employees to answer the same questions repeatedly.

Think of a Media Kit like a 'resume' for your brand.

Besides having a Media Kit to send to Brands, the benefits of having a Media Kit are:
- It gives people a snapshot into your Brand
- Helps establish credibility by showing what type of content you've created, where you may have been featured, and what brands you may have partnered with in the past
- Create brand awareness by visually seeing the aesthetics of your brand
- Opens the space for growth and partnership opportunities.

When creating your Media Kit, you want to make sure that you have pertinent information there that gives the viewer what they need and captures their attention within the first seven seconds.

Some of the essential elements to include are:
- Company Overview + Brand Story + Bio
- Who You Serve + WHY
- Facts Sheet
- Samples +/or Offerings
- Testimonials + Press
- Graphics, visuals, or links to videos you have created
- Contact Information

Lastly, make sure your Media Kit is visually appealing and is 'on brand.' This is your 'portfolio,' so you want to make sure it is as closely aligned as possible.

You can get the **Media Kit** template that I've used for years to land tons of collaborations by going here: www.RachelTravels.com/Media-Kit-Template/

How To Effectively Pitch Brands

After you have created your Media Kit, you are now ready to pitch and secure your first partnership! Here are the steps to follow to do this:

Step #1: Understanding What You Are Asking For:

Before reaching out to Brands, you must do research and understand what the goals and objectives are for the brand. You can do this by:
- Reading the company's press releases
- Follow them on social media and understand what they are currently promoting
- Glance at their Vision/ Mission statements and see if your brand is in alignment
- Researching the company on a site like LinkedIn

Once you understand what the brand is seeking, come up with 3-5 ways you can help them achieve their goals.

Before contacting a Brand, ask yourself "How is this mutually beneficial?"

Be crystal clear on what you are seeking in a partnership, collaboration, or sponsorship with another brand.

- Are you looking for a complimentary stay in a hotel in exchange for a review?
- Would you like to create content for a brand in the form of high- quality images and video
- Is becoming a Brand Ambassador something you would want to pitch?

There are many options, but you must be clear on your goals, what the brand is seeking, and how you can meet the brand's needs.

Step #2: Find the Right Contacts to Pitch

Even if you have the most beautiful Media Kit and a solid pitch letter, it will all be in vain, if you don't find the right contacts to send your pitch.

Here are four easy ways to find the right contacts to land your first travel partnership:

1) **Use The Site Map**: With larger brands (like hotels chains, big franchises, etc.), you want to search their site to see who the listed contacts are on there. Start in the "Contact" area or the Site Map. If you see a Public Relations or Marketing Manager contact listed, then this is who you want to pitch first. If it is a smaller brand and a Manager (or owner) is listed, then contact them directly.

2) **Ask For the Right Contact**: One of the easiest and quickest ways to find the right contact is to ask straight out. If you're active on social media, send tweets or direct messages (DM) to the Brand and ask who you should be contacting.

A simple message could read like this:

Hello! I am _____ a travel [blogger, podcaster, vlogger, influencer, etc.]. I would love to a partner with [insert name of property/tour/restaurant/ tourism board/etc.]. Who is the right person to contact for this? Thanks!

3) **Google Is Your Bestie**: While this strategy takes a bit more work, it is a great place to start and see who works with Travel Influencers. By law, content creators have to disclose and credit whoever sponsored or compensated them in exchange for social media exposure. Typically, the disclosure statement is similar. Use this to your advantage and reverse engineer, to find content creators who have partnered with Brands for collaborations.

Here's an example: if you are looking to find hotels in Paris, France that has worked with Influencers in the past, then do the following: Google "all opinions are my own" "[insert name of city]" (hotel, tour, restaurant, etc.)

Search: 'all opinions are my own' 'Paris' 'hotel.'

Now read through the search result. The content creator has mentioned the specific hotel or brand they have worked with for that content piece. Create a list of these hotels and pitch them directly.

You are saving time and effort by not aimlessly pitching brands that may or may not work with Travel Influencers.

4) **Leverage LinkedIn**: Surprisingly, many people do not mention this method of finding the right contacts for securing your first travel sponsorship. LinkedIn is such a great resource. Here is also an opportunity to read more about the organization, what their mission is, the latest projects they are working on, achievements,

awards, how long they've been around, and so on. Leverage this information to your advantage.

Once you've found the Brand, you would like to work with, take some time to search and find the Manager, PR Representative, Marketing Manager. Send them a message on LinkedIn.

Using these five methods, you will surely be able to find the right contacts to land your first travel partnerships. However, finding the right connections is just the very beginning of the pitching process.

Step #3: Go In For The Pitch:

There are two ways to approach this:
1) Send an Introduction Email
a.   You can use mine here:
https://racheltravels.com/shop-cart/templates
2) Direct Pitch

Now that you are clear on what the brand is looking for, what would be mutually beneficial from the partnership, and how to find the right contacts, your next step is going in for the pitch.

Below is a sample pitch you can use:

Hello ___

My name is [insert name], founder/creator/blogger at [insert name of your brand].

I have been a loyal [fan/customer/subscriber/etc.] to _____ for some time now.

I love the [insert project/program/product] that the company has created. I admire [insert something you respect and appreciate about what the company is doing].
I noticed you are an advocate for [insert something that means a lot to the Brand or an initiative they're working on].

[In 2-3 sentences, describe how your brand aligns, and you can help them spread said message].

Let me know how I can support you and this initiative.

I am looking forward to hearing from you soon.

Sign Your Name

Contact
Social Media Handles

If you want a bundle of the pitch templates I have been using for years and a training video, then you can grab **The Pitch Template Bundle**: https://www.racheltravels.com/shop-cart/templates

HACK: Work With Similar Smaller Brands Then Scale Up To Bigger Brands:

If you are starting pitching brands, then begin with smaller brands. It's much easier and more accessible to work with brands that have a similar following to you so that you can both partner together and scale up by leveraging each other's audiences.

What You Should Be Charging Brands:

Many people get stuck here. When you are getting ready to ask for monetary compensation, you must understand your worth to a brand. There is no exact formula. And unfortunately, there also is no right or wrong way to approach this concept.

To get an idea of where to start charging, utilize this site as a resource and starting point:
- **Social Bluebook**: https://socialbluebook.com/

You have the option of going up in cost by creating "packages" of what you can or are willing to offer the brands; like featuring the product/service in your live videos, adding it to your daily video stories, multiple posts on multiple platforms.

HACK: Create a Rate Card

A rate card is a document detailing prices for various services and placement options.

This is fantastic to diversify your brand and generate more money from working with brands. If a brand offers to pay you just for a sponsored post, you can send them your Rate Card.

This is a great way to add more value to the partnering company and earn more income. The more services or offerings you add to the packages, the higher the cost. It is essential to make each package more and more valuable.

Add-ons Can Include:
- Written content
- Live Videos/ Stories
- Social Media Shares
- Curated Video
- High- quality Images
- Your Email List

There is a Sample Rate Card in the **Pitch Template Bundle**:
https://www.racheltravels.com/shop-cart/templates

CHAPTER NINE

Travel Influence As A Business

The Importance of Investing In Yourself As A Business

Let's cover a topic that many often shy away from when it comes to being a profitable Travel Influencer: Mindset + Money.

You must be prepared to charge, more specifically, charge what you are worth.

In the beginning, it can be intimidating and seem difficult to charge for something you are passionate about, in order to take your brand to the next level, you must have offerings that you monetize consistently.

Mindset is everything.

For many of us, it feels utterly uncomfortable in the beginning because we are not used to charging what we would so happily discuss or talk about for $FREE.99.

When preparing to monetize some of your content, here are a few mindset exercises you can use to help shift your perspective:
- Say or read affirmations about your worthiness daily.
- Read books about clearing money blocks
- Write out a list of all of the things you are highly knowledgeable and skilled in and understand why people would pay for this.
- Start off by offering smaller price point items between the $7-47 range.

Think about it. Compared to the free things you receive and that which you purchase - which do you take more seriously?

"Charge your worth and add tax." – Instagram Proverb

Your time, effort, and expertise are worth it.

Business Expenses You Should Account For:

As a profitable Travel Influencer, you must understand, you are *running a business*. Which means on top of monetizing your content, you will incur business and operating expenses.

While there is a long list to consider, as you begin your endeavor as an Influencer, there are business expenses that you should be aware of very early on. Here are three of them to take into account:

TAXES

You know the saying, "The only two things that are certain in this world: Dying and paying taxes." You see the government, no matter where you live in this world, is going to make sure they get a cut of your hard work. It is what it is.

While we are not in an immediate position to change this, we need to be aware that taxes are *real*. Make sure you put money aside for taxes. You do not want to get to the end of the year when it is time to file and pay taxes, and you end up owing a ton.

OPERATING EXPENSES

Create a budget and a line-item list of the amount of money needed monthly to manage your business. One of the amazing things about running an online brand is that the overhead is very low.

In the beginning, your operating expenses may include:

- **Website**: You may be paying monthly for a site or a hosting service.
- **Payment Gateway Fees**: If you use services like, PayPal or Stripe, you will incur fees per transaction.
- **Email List Software**: If you have a growing email list, you will have to pay for the service, especially for the more robust features, like automation, segmenting, and tagging. Many start free, but you will eventually upgrade for more robust features and functionality.
  Social Media Management Software: If you use programs that easily automate your content, then you will likely have to pay for the advanced features and functionality.
- **Accounting Software**: You want to include software that helps you manage your expenses and gives you an idea of what to pay in taxes at the end of the year.

- **Shipping + Courier Services**: If you are shipping out physical products, then you will incur shipping costs and pay for services that will make the fulfillment process manageable.

Each business is different, but you want to make sure that you understand what these expenses are, so you can make sure you are earning enough monthly to cover operating expenses and make a <u>profit</u>.

ADVERTISING BUDGET

The cost of advertising should be in your budget. In the beginning, you may be uncomfortable or unsure about utilizing paid advertising. However, be assured that this is something you want to eventually start accounting for, especially if you want your business as a Travel Influencer to take off quickly.

Tools for Consistent Profit:

Making money on autopilot (i.e., "money while you're asleep"), is a lot easier than you think.

It takes a strategy, the right systems, and setting them up to run on their own.

Here are three tools you will need in place to start making consistent income on autopilot:

TOOL #1: A SCHEDULING TOOL

One of the first tools you will need in place is scheduling software to make sure that people 24/365 are seeing your content. Talk about consistency! There are many social media scheduling tools on the market.

Once you have your product offerings in place, you will be able the content and schedule them within your software so people can be introduced to your content and paid products/services 24/7.

TOOL #2: EMAIL MARKETING SYSTEM

Email Marketing was discussed earlier in this book. To begin to generate consistent income, you MUST have an email marketing system in place.

There are plenty of free versions to start with as you begin. As your brand grows, you will eventually need to upgrade to the paid versions, which offer more robust and functional systems.

TOOL #3: PAYMENT GATEWAY

Lastly, to make a consistent income, you have to have an outlet to receive payments. There is entirely no way that you can make a consistent profit and revenue if you have no way to take payments.

There are many ways to accept payments; however, the easiest to set up is a Stripe account or PayPal.

How To Make Sales On Autopilot:

Utilizing the tools in the previous section, here is a step-by-step guide on how to create sales on autopilot. The idea of sales on autopilot is to give away something super valuable for free, then convince your audience to purchase a paid product or service from you. All of this is done without you physically having to pitch or launch all day every day.

The steps are:

STEP #1: CREATE A FREEBIE

Under "Monetizing Your Influence," you learned how to create a product. For this freebie, create a small offer like a checklist, template, or guide that you are willing to give away for free. For your audience to receive your freebie (also known as an 'opt-in,' 'lead magnet,' or 'lead gen'), create a "sign up" form. You can quickly create one from the email marketing software that you are currently utilizing.

Note: On the signup form, only ask for first name and email. Some studies have shown that you may get a higher conversion rate if you ask for only emails.

STEP #2: EMAIL FUNNEL

Utilizing the email marketing system, you will create what is called an auto-responder. This means, when someone submits their name and email to you through the "signup form," they will automatically be sent an email from you via the from the email system.

Using the AutoResponder, you will create a series of three to five emails.

This is what is called a "Sales Funnel."

Deep diving into the science and theory of a Sales Funnel is outside the scope of this book; however, it is highly encouraged to study the various types of Sales Funnels, as there are many that work for different business models.

Here is How A Simple Sales Funnel May Look:

Email 1: Autoresponder Welcome Message

Email 2: Share Something Educational or Give A Tip or Hack
Ex: "3 Ways to Travel On a Budget."

Email 3: Share Facts
Ex: "5 Ways to Save On International Travel"

Email 4: Warm Them Up With Previews of Your Paid Product or Service
Ex: "How I Was Able to Go to Colombia for $121".

Email 5: Pitch Your Product or Service!

STEP #3: HOW TO PITCH TO SELL

The fifth email is the email that you will use to pitch your product or service. Here is a sample email, that has worked well with converting into sales:

Hey [first name]

Are you having difficulties with any of these?

[Ask them 3-5 questions that you know they have concerns or confusion about]

I get it.

I'm sure you may think [insert a limitation].

You want to do more _____ and _____, however, you're not sure where to start.

Well, that is why I/we created [insert offering of paid product/service].

After taking/doing [Offering], you will know how to:

- What They Will Learn
- What They Will Learn
- What They Will Learn

The [Offering] Includes:

- Benefit Customer Will Take Away
- Benefit Customer Will Take Away
- Benefit Customer Will Take Away
- BONUS #1:
- BONUS #2:

The investment in [Offering] is only $_____.

>> CLICK HERE TO SIGN UP FOR [Offering} and grab the bonuses!

Still not sure if this is right for your [first name].
Reply to this email with any questions or concerns.

Signed,

[Your Name]

Consider learning how to write copy in a way that is created to convert sales.

Many of the things you read have trigger words and phrases, which subconsciously make you, desire a product or service even more. This is effective copywriting.

Learning how to write effectively and convincing copy is both art and science. Nonetheless, it is something that anyone can learn how to do quite easily.
For now, you have the fundamentals of what it takes to be a profitable Travel Influencer!

CHAPTER TEN

Final Thoughts

Your journey toward building a profitable brand as a Travel Influencer will ebb and flow. There are going to be high moments, and there are going to be some moments where you will be unclear, overwhelmed, and frustrated.

Enjoy the journey.

Build your brand by your own terms, in your own lane, and in your uniqueness.

Those times were get you may get discouraged, here is what you do:
Remember why you wanted to become a Travel Influencer.
If it is for the right reasons, which is to change the perception of how your audience views how travel is transformative – then this will help you stay focused and motivated.

Egypt was not built in a day.

You are more than capable of building a business by doing what you love. It takes time, consistency, and dedication – everything after this, will fall into place.

Be patient. Create a goal and work towards it.

RACHEL ✈ TRAVELS

About The Author

Rachel V. Hill is an Influencer Marketing Expert from Orlando, FL.

After silently suffering from Anxiety Disorder and Depression, Rachel "retired" from Corporate America at 27, to travel the world indefinitely.

Initially starting RachelTravels.com as an open journal for her solo journey, backpacking journey through SE Asia, she soon saw there was a gap in the narrative of what it means to be a Black Traveler. She has then created a platform to serve this demographic and more.

Within four years, through creative and digital strategy, she created a travel brand with thousands of followers that influences and inspires millennial of color to push past their comfort zones and travel the world.
To hire Rachel for Corporate Consulting and Training please contact:
Rachel@RachelTravels.com.

To learn more about her course, programs, + to work more with Rachel, visit: www.RachelTravels.com .

RESOURCES

FAVORITE TOOLS

SOCIAL MEDIA:

SmarterQueue.com: Automate your Social Media
Get 30 Days FREE On Me! → http://bit.ly/rtsmarterqueue

Later.com: Schedule Your Social Media Posts Like Instagram, Facebook, and Pinterest

EMAIL SYSTEMS:

Mailchimp.com: Email marketing system that includes features like automation, segmenting, and more!
→ FREEMIUM Version Here: http://bit.ly/rtmailchimp (case sensitive)

SCHEDULING:

Acuity.com: Allow people to make payments to consult with you or schedule services. I've been using this service for years to schedule "Coffee Dates" or consulting sessions.
→ FREE Trial On Me: http://bit.ly/rtacuity (case sensitive)

OUTSOURCING:

Fiverr.com: Outsource tasks starting at $5!
→ Your First Gig FREE On Me: http://bit.ly/rtfiverr (case sensitive)

HOME SHARING (for extra income):

AirBnB.com: A great way to travel and generate passive income from your home!
→ FREE Stay On Me: http://bit.ly/rtairbnb (case sensitive)

30 Content Ideas

Desired Result: Over the next thirty days, use this outline to create enough content for at least two months.
Time: 30 - 60 mins/ Day

CHOOSE A PLATFORM:
Day 1: Write A Bio
Day 2: Mind Mapping
Day 3: How Often Will You Post Strategy Plan
Day 4: Decide which two platforms you'll post on most often
Day 5: Sign up for a site like SmarterQueue
Day 6: Write about your mission and vision for your platform
Day 7: Write out Five Goals for Platform
Day 8: Create Categories for Your Platform (At least three)
Day 9: Create A Page for Links or Open a Linktree Account (I don't 100% recommend LinkTree)
Day 10: Create a video introducing yourself to your audience

CONTENT:
Day 11: Write 10 Possible Post Ideas (Refer to Day 8)
Day 12: Write 10 Possible Post Ideas (Refer to Day 8)
Day 13: Research & Find Five People to Interview or Collaborate With
Day 14: Create a Bucket Life List Post
Day 15: Use http://buzzsumo.com/ to generate some trending ideas
Day 16: Brainstorm Five Ideas for Listicles (Ex:"10 Things You Should...", "7 Destinations To...")
Day 17: Tell Your Story
Day 18: Brainstorm 10 Ideas for Travel Guides
Day 19: Brainstorm Three Ideas for a "Stop Guide" (ex: "How to Stop Paying So Much to Travel."
Day 20: Create Five Ideas of Things You Want to Sell

SOCIAL MEDIA:

Day 21: Create a Posting Strategy for Your Social Media

Day 22: Download & Learn Editing Apps

Day 23: Develop Five "Call-to-Action" sentences that you can use (this would pair well with Day 20) (Ex: "Interested in learning how to travel like a boss? Click the link in the Bio!")

Day 24: Find 5-10 #TBT photos and write out captions for it

Day 25: Ask people to Join your Mailing List (Tools Page)

Day 26: Create Three "Behind the Scenes" posts

Day 27: GO LIVE + Share Your Freebie/ Opt-in

Day 28: Share Your Freebie/ Opt-in

Day 29: Develop Five Questions to Ask Your Audience

Day 30: GO LIVE!

ENDNOTES

[I] "Multicultural Marketing: No Longer an Option, But a Necessity"
https://www.inc.com/yuriy-boykiv/multicultural-marketing-no-longer-an-option-but-a-necessity.html

[II] "Black Impact: Consumer Categories Where African Americans Move Markets",
https://www.nielsen.com/us/en/insights/news/2018/black-impact-consumer-categories-where-african-americans-move-markets.html

[III] "Black Impact: Consumer Categories Where African Americans Move Markets",
https://www.nielsen.com/us/en/insights/news/2018/black-impact-consumer-categories-where-african-americans-move-markets.html

[IV] "Black Impact: Consumer Categories Where African Americans Move Markets",
https://www.nielsen.com/us/en/insights/news/2018/black-impact-consumer-categories-where-african-americans-move-markets.html

27774893R00066

Made in the USA
San Bernardino, CA
03 March 2019